# MY FIRST

# BATTERIES & MAGNETS
## B·O·O·K

JACK CHALLONER

**DORLING KINDERSLEY**
London • New York • Stuttgart

A Dorling Kindersley Book

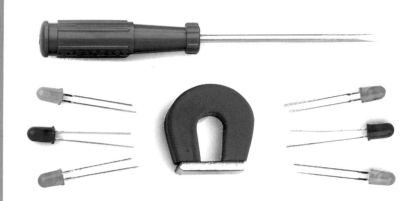

**Design** *Penny Britchfield*
**Editor** *Helen Drew*
**Photography** *Dave King*
**Production** *Norina Bremner*

**Managing Editor** *Jane Yorke*
**Managing Art Editor** *Chris Scollen*

First published in Great Britain in 1992
by Dorling Kindersley Limited, London
9 Henrietta Street, London WC2E 8PS
Reprinted in 1994

**A CIP catalogue record for this book
is available from the British Library**

ISBN 086318-895-8

Phototypeset by The Setting Studio, Newcastle
Colour reproduction by Colourscan, Singapore
Printed and bound in Italy by L.E.G.O.

Dorling Kindersley would like to thank Jonathan Buckley,
Mandy Earey, Westley Kirton, Jane Bull and Peter Radcliffe for their
help in producing this book.

Illustrations by Brian Delf

# CONTENTS

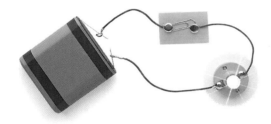

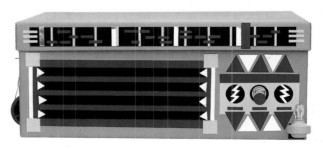

# SCIENCE BY PICTURES

*My First Batteries & Magnets Book* is full of exciting science projects to do at home, that will help you to find out more about electricity and magnetism. Step-by-step photographs and simple instructions show you exactly what to do, and there are life-size photographs of everything you need to collect and of the finished projects. On the opposite page is a list of things to remember when using this book, and below you can find out what to look for in each experiment.

## How to use this book

**What the project is about**
The introduction to each project tells you important information about the activity shown.

**The things you need**
The things to collect for each project are shown life-size to help you check that you have everything you need.

**Step-by-step**
Step-by-step photographs and clear instructions tell you exactly what to do at each stage of the project.

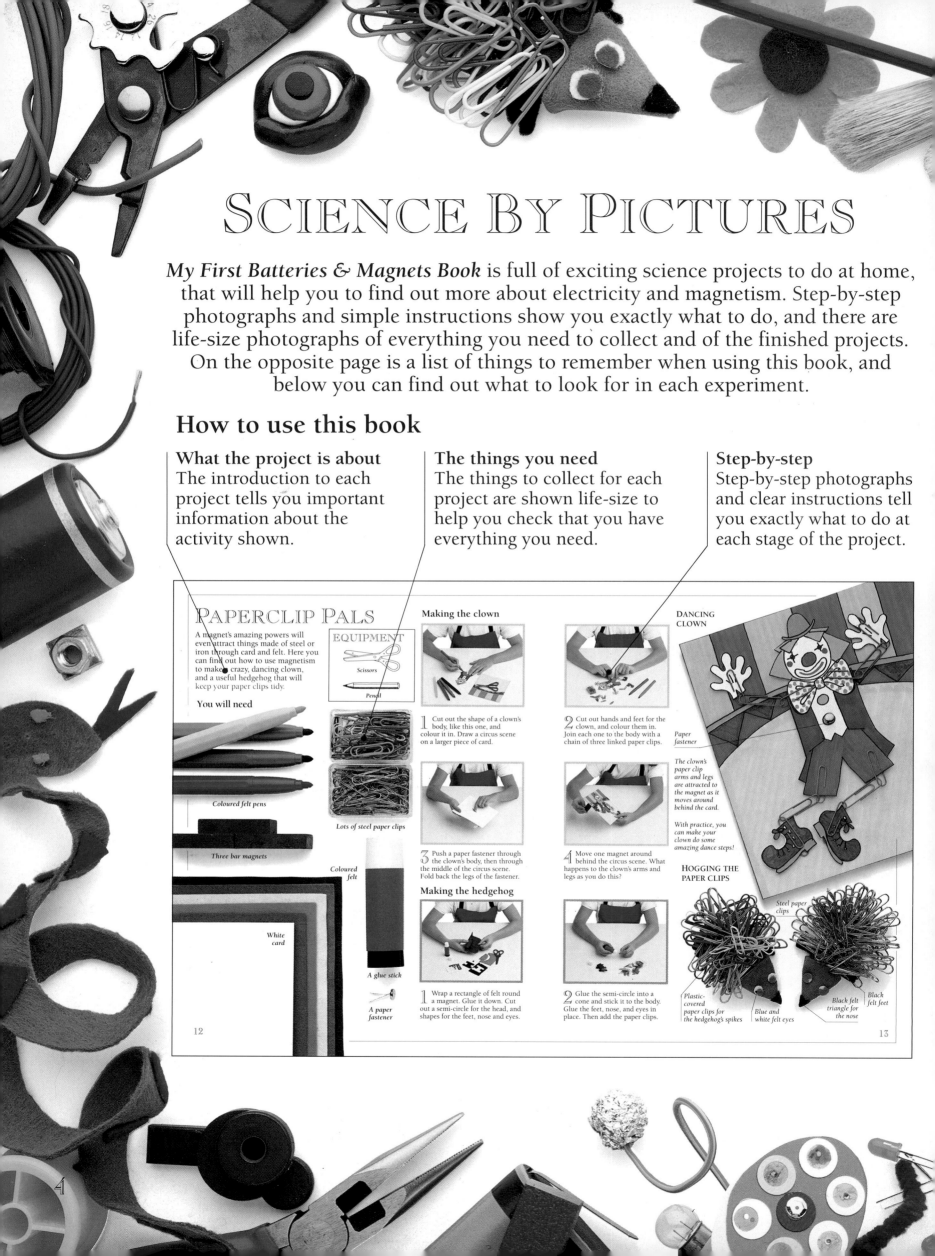

### PAPERCLIP PALS

A magnet's amazing powers will even attract things made of steel or iron through card and felt. Here you can find out how to use magnetism to make a crazy, dancing clown, and a useful hedgehog that will keep your paper clips tidy.

**You will need**

EQUIPMENT

*Scissors*

*Pencil*

*Coloured felt pens*

*Lots of steel paper clips*

*Three bar magnets*

*Coloured felt*

*White card*

*A glue stick*

*A paper fastener*

**Making the clown**

1 Cut out the shape of a clown's body, like this one, and colour it in. Draw a circus scene on a larger piece of card.

2 Cut out hands and feet for the clown, and colour them in. Join each one to the body with a chain of three linked paper clips.

3 Push a paper fastener through the clown's body, then through the middle of the circus scene. Fold back the legs of the fastener.

4 Move one magnet around behind the circus scene. What happens to the clown's arms and legs as you do this?

**Making the hedgehog**

1 Wrap a rectangle of felt round a magnet. Glue it down. Cut out a semi-circle for the head, and shapes for the feet, nose and eyes.

2 Glue the semi-circle into a cone and stick it to the body. Glue the feet, nose, and eyes in place. Then add the paper clips.

**DANCING CLOWN**

*Paper fastener*

*The clown's paper clip arms and legs are attracted to the magnet as it moves around behind the card.*

*With practice, you can make your clown do some amazing dance steps!*

**HOGGING THE PAPER CLIPS**

*Steel paper clips*

*Plastic-covered paper clips for the hedgehog's spikes*

*Blue and white felt eyes*

*Black felt triangle for the nose*

12

13

# Things to remember

**1** **Always use batteries in the projects in this book. Never use electricity from the wall sockets, as it is very dangerous.**

**2** Read the instructions before you start and gather together everything you need for the project.

**3** Be very careful when using wire strippers, scissors, and screwdrivers. **Do not use them unless an adult is there to help.**

**4** Try not to drop your magnets, as they may lose their magnetism. You can remagnetise them a little by stroking them in one direction with another magnet (see page 17).

**5** Always turn off battery-powered projects when you are not using them, as batteries may get hot, or run down.

**6** When you have finished, put your project away safely, then clean up and put away everything you have used.

**Equipment**
Illustrated checklists show you which tools you will need to have ready before you start each project.

**The finished results**
Colourful life-sized photographs show you what happens in each experiment and what the finished project looks like.

**Useful explanations**
At the end of each project you will find clear explanations of what is happening, and why.

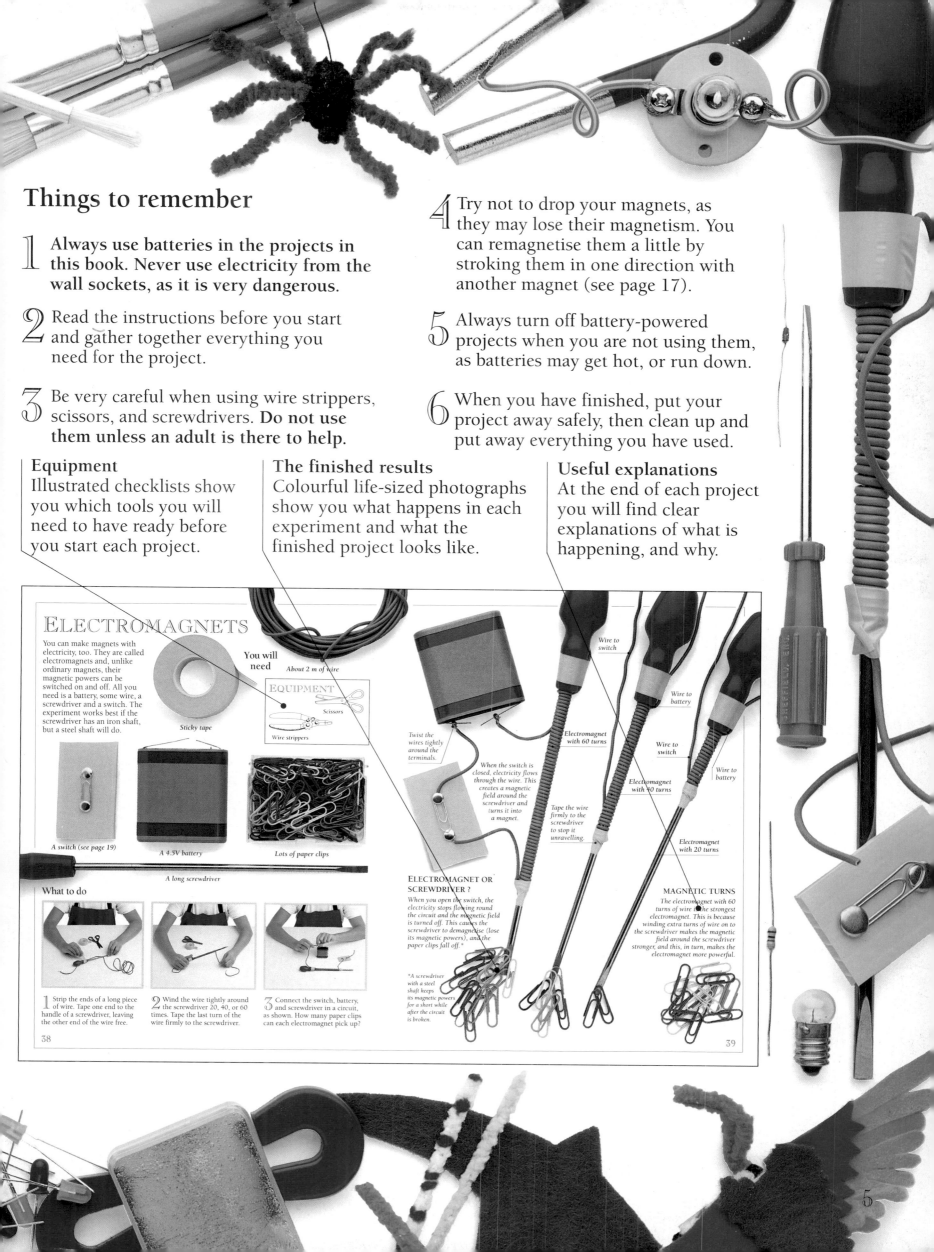

## ELECTROMAGNETS

You can make magnets with electricity, too. They are called electromagnets and, unlike ordinary magnets, their magnetic powers can be switched on and off. All you need is a battery, some wire, a screwdriver and a switch. The experiment works best if the screwdriver has an iron shaft, but a steel shaft will do.

Sticky tape

**You will need** About 2 m of wire

**EQUIPMENT**
Scissors
Wire strippers

A switch (see page 19)

A 4.5V battery

Lots of paper clips

A long screwdriver

### What to do

**1** Strip the ends of a long piece of wire. Tape one end to the handle of a screwdriver, leaving the other end of the wire free.

**2** Wind the wire tightly around the screwdriver 20, 40, or 60 times. Tape the last turn of the wire firmly to the screwdriver.

**3** Connect the switch, battery and screwdriver in a circuit, as shown. How many paper clips can each electromagnet pick up?

Twist the wires tightly around the terminals.

When the switch is closed, electricity flows through the wire. This creates a magnetic field around the screwdriver and turns it into a magnet.

Wire to switch

Wire to battery

Electromagnet with 60 turns

Wire to switch

Tape the wire firmly to the screwdriver to stop it unravelling.

Electromagnet with 40 turns

Wire to battery

Electromagnet with 20 turns

### ELECTROMAGNET OR SCREWDRIVER?

When you open the switch, the electricity stops flowing round the circuit and the magnetic field is turned off. This causes the screwdriver to demagnetise (lose its magnetic powers), and the paper clips fall off.*

*A screwdriver with a steel shaft keeps its magnetic powers for a short while after the circuit is broken.

### MAGNETIC TURNS

The electromagnet with 60 turns of wire is the strongest electromagnet. This is because winding extra turns of wire on to the screwdriver makes the magnetic field around the screwdriver stronger, and this, in turn, makes the electromagnet more powerful.

38

39

# Batteries And Magnets Kit

Here you can see the special tools and equipment you will need to make the projects in this book. Page 48 has lots of tips on where to buy them.

Batteries, bulbs and electronic components come in many different sizes, so be careful to buy the right ones.

*A 9V (9 Volt) battery*

*A 1.5V battery*

*A 4.5V battery*

*Small electric motors (1.5V-4V)*

*1.5V, 2.5V, 3.5V and 4.5V bulbs*

*Bulb holders*

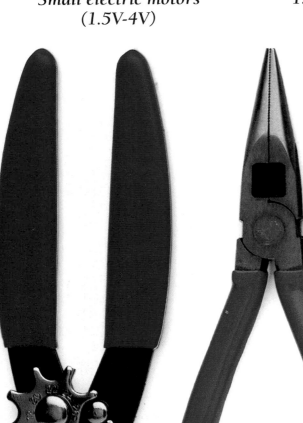

*Wire strippers*

*Pliers*

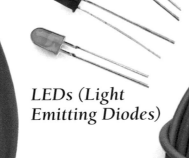

*A variable resistor*

*Lots of plastic-coated flex*

**Electronic components for the transistor radio (see pages 42-43)**

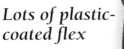

*LEDs (Light Emitting Diodes)*

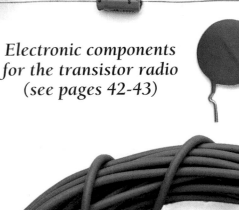

*An earphone for radio (sometimes called a crystal earpiece)*

Bar magnets

Square magnets

Round magnets

Horseshoe magnets

Iron filings

Small screwdrivers

Metal paper clips

A cross-head
screwdriver

Metal paper
fasteners

Corrugated
plastic or
cardboard

Sticky tape

Aluminium
foil

Scissors

7

# MAGIC MAGNETS

Magnets have special powers that seem to be magic. Their power is called magnetism, and it can move certain objects around without even touching them. Below you can find out more about your magnet, then use its powers to do some exciting tricks.

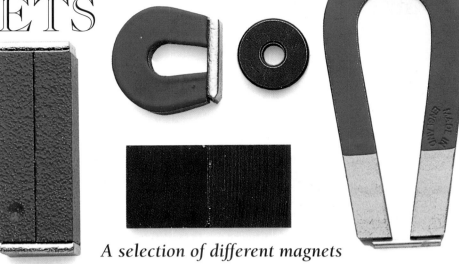

*A selection of different magnets*

*A variety of small household objects and steel paper clips*

## You will need

*Snake pattern*

*A ruler*

*Cotton thread*

*Pieces of coloured felt*

*Glue*

*Sticky tape*

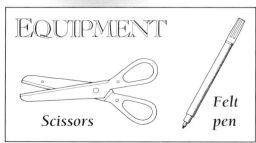

EQUIPMENT

*Scissors*

*Felt pen*

## Magnetic attraction

Hold a magnet close to each of the objects you have collected. Which objects does the magnet pick up? What are they made of?

8

# Making the snake

**1** Trace the snake pattern on the opposite page, then cut it out in felt. Decorate your snake with small pieces of coloured felt.

**2** Give the snake felt eyes and a tongue. Tie a short piece of thread to a paper clip. Slide the paper clip on to the snake's head.

**3** Tape a magnet to one end of the ruler. Tape the thread from the snake firmly to the table, as shown.

## It's magnetic magic!

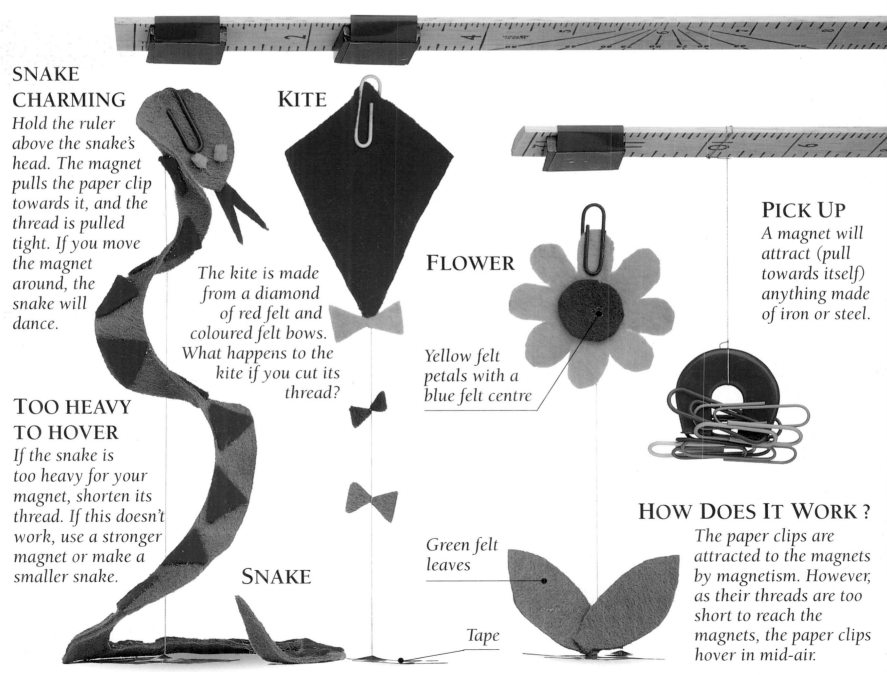

### SNAKE CHARMING
*Hold the ruler above the snake's head. The magnet pulls the paper clip towards it, and the thread is pulled tight. If you move the magnet around, the snake will dance.*

### KITE
*The kite is made from a diamond of red felt and coloured felt bows. What happens to the kite if you cut its thread?*

### TOO HEAVY TO HOVER
*If the snake is too heavy for your magnet, shorten its thread. If this doesn't work, use a stronger magnet or make a smaller snake.*

**SNAKE**

**FLOWER**

*Yellow felt petals with a blue felt centre*

*Green felt leaves*

*Tape*

### PICK UP
*A magnet will attract (pull towards itself) anything made of iron or steel.*

### HOW DOES IT WORK?
*The paper clips are attracted to the magnets by magnetism. However, as their threads are too short to reach the magnets, the paper clips hover in mid-air.*

9

# FRIDGE MAGNETS

Brighten up your kitchen with colourful decorations that cling to the fridge! Fridge magnets can come in all shapes and sizes and they are very easy to make. The magnets stick to the outside of the fridge, because it is made of steel. Try sticking them to other metal things around your home.

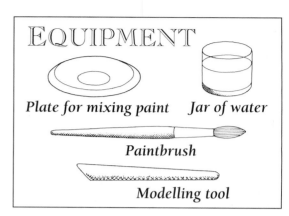
## You will need

*Coloured oven-hardening clay**

*Clear nail varnish*

*Poster paints*

*Plain self-hardening clay*

*Glue*

*Small, flat magnets*

## What to do

1 Model any shape you like out of clay. Harden your shapes by following the instructions on the clay packet very carefully.

2 Paint the shapes made of plain clay and leave them to dry. Brush all of your shapes with clear nail varnish.

3 When the varnish is dry, glue a magnet to the back of each shape. Once the glue has set, the fridge magnets are ready to use.

*Ask an adult to help you to harden shapes made from this clay.

# Magnetic fridge friends

*The whale and the monster were made from coloured oven-hardening clays and the acrobats, fish, and dinosaur from plain, self-hardening clay, which was painted.*

**MAGNETIC MINNOWS**

**WALLY**

**MONSTER ATTRACTION**

**DINOSAUR ON DUTY**
*Make an army of your favourite dinosaurs to guard the fridge!*

**ACROBATIC ADVENTURE**
*Arrange your acrobats in incredible balancing positions.*

# Paper Clip Pals

A magnet's amazing powers will even attract things made of steel or iron through card and felt. Here you can find out how to use magnetism to make a crazy, dancing clown, and a useful hedgehog that will keep your paper clips tidy.

## You will need

*Coloured felt pens*

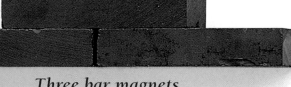

*Three bar magnets*

### EQUIPMENT

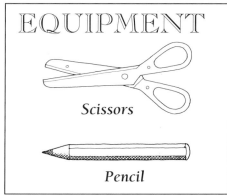

*Scissors*

*Pencil*

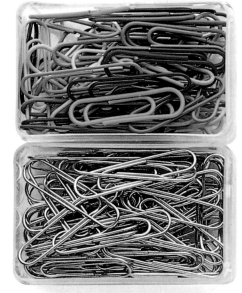

*Lots of steel paper clips*

*Coloured felt*

*White card*

*A glue stick*

*A paper fastener*

## Making the clown

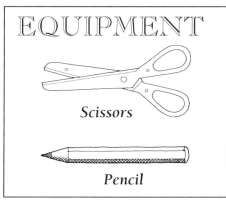

1 Cut out the shape of a clown's body, like this one, and colour it in. Draw a circus scene on a larger piece of card.

3 Push a paper fastener through the clown's body, then through the middle of the circus scene. Fold back the legs of the fastener.

## Making the hedgehog

1 Wrap a rectangle of felt round a magnet. Glue it down. Cut out a semi-circle for the head, and shapes for the feet, nose and eyes.

12

2 Cut out hands and feet for the clown, and colour them in. Join each one to the body with a chain of three linked paper clips.

4 Move one magnet around behind the circus scene. What happens to the clown's arms and legs as you do this?

2 Glue the semi-circle into a cone and stick it to the body. Glue the feet, nose, and eyes in place. Then add the paper clips.

## DANCING CLOWN

*Paper fastener*

*The clown's paper clip arms and legs are attracted to the magnet as it moves around behind the card.*

*With practice, you can make your clown do some amazing dance steps!*

## HOGGING THE PAPER CLIPS

*Steel paper clips*

*Plastic-covered paper clips for the hedgehog's spikes*

*Blue and white felt eyes*

*Black felt triangle for the nose*

*Black felt feet*

# MAGNETIC FIELDS

A magnet's invisible powers are contained within its 'magnetic field'. You can see the pattern of a magnetic field by putting iron filings near a magnet. Iron filings usually leap towards a magnet, but if you put them in sticky syrup, they will form magnetic patterns very slowly. Stir up the filings in the syrup, every time you use the mixture.

## EQUIPMENT

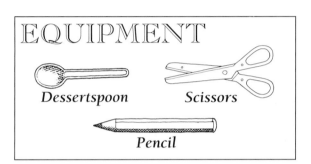

*Dessertspoon*  *Scissors*

*Pencil*

## You will need

*A selection of different magnets*

*Some string*

*Iron filings*

*Clear plastic tubs or glass containers*

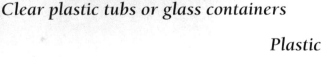

*Golden syrup*

*Plastic wrap*

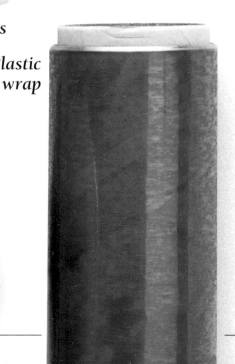

## Making the mixture

Sprinkle a dessertspoonful of iron filings into the syrup. Stir gently until the iron filings are evenly mixed into the syrup.

## Magnetic patterns

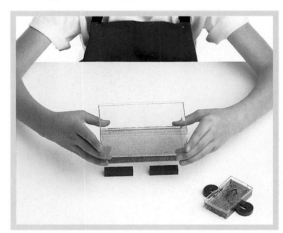

Pour some mixture into each tub. Place magnets underneath or at the sides of the tubs, then watch as the magnetic fields appear.

## 3-D fields

Fill a glass with mixture. Cover a bar magnet in plastic wrap, and tie it to a pencil with string. Hang the magnet in the middle of the glass.

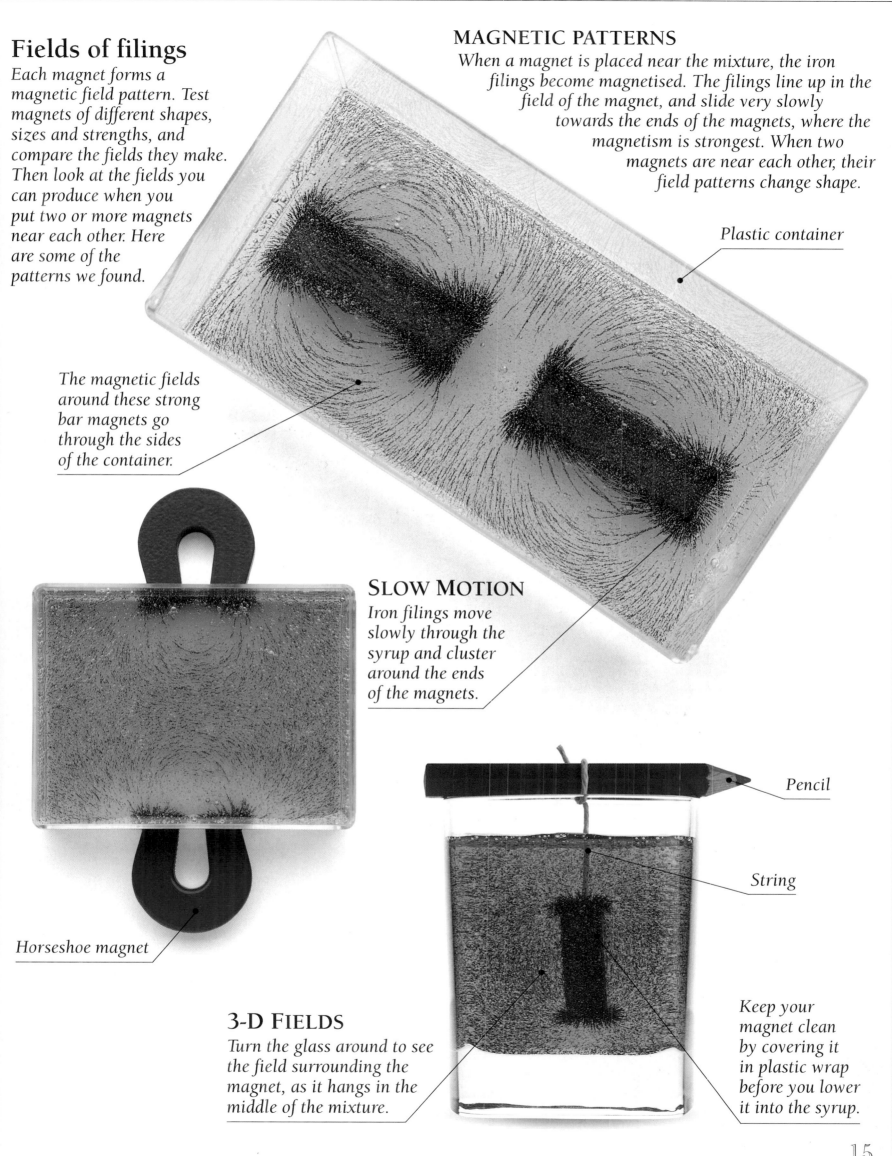

# Fields of filings

*Each magnet forms a magnetic field pattern. Test magnets of different shapes, sizes and strengths, and compare the fields they make. Then look at the fields you can produce when you put two or more magnets near each other. Here are some of the patterns we found.*

## MAGNETIC PATTERNS

*When a magnet is placed near the mixture, the iron filings become magnetised. The filings line up in the field of the magnet, and slide very slowly towards the ends of the magnets, where the magnetism is strongest. When two magnets are near each other, their field patterns change shape.*

Plastic container

*The magnetic fields around these strong bar magnets go through the sides of the container.*

## SLOW MOTION

Iron filings move slowly through the syrup and cluster around the ends of the magnets.

Horseshoe magnet

Pencil

String

## 3-D FIELDS

*Turn the glass around to see the field surrounding the magnet, as it hangs in the middle of the mixture.*

*Keep your magnet clean by covering it in plastic wrap before you lower it into the syrup.*

15

# POLES APART

Every magnet has a north pole and a south pole, like the Earth. These poles are the two opposite ends, or sides, of a magnet, where its powers are strongest. You can find out more about magnetic poles, how to identify them and why magnets behave oddly when they are together, in the experiments below. Opposite you can see how to make your own magnets, as well as an amazing turtle compass that really works.

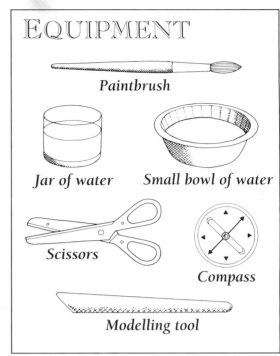

*Poster paint*

*A bottle top*

## EQUIPMENT

*Paintbrush*

*Jar of water*

*Small bowl of water*

*Scissors*

*Compass*

*Modelling tool*

*Wooden skewers*

*A steel needle*

## You will need

*A horseshoe magnet*

*Coloured modelling clay*

*Strong bar magnets*

*Ring magnets*

## North or south pole?

Hang a bar magnet above the compass, as shown*. When it stops moving, the end pointing north is the magnet's north pole.

## Pole position

Try pushing the north poles, then the south poles of two magnets together. What happens? Next, try a north and a south pole together.

## Making the lion

Paint some skewers, cut them in half, and stick them in some clay around a bar magnet. Model a clay lion. Sit it on another bar magnet.

## Making the clown

Stick three skewers into some clay. Put some ring magnets onto the skewers. Model a clown from clay, and stick it on the top magnet.

16

*\* The magnet will affect the compass needle if it is too close.*

# Turtle compass

1 Stroke a needle, 30 times from its point to its eye, with the south pole of a magnet. Make a light, flat turtle from clay.

2 Push the turtle onto the open end of the bottle top. Stick the needle point firmly into the turtle's tail, directly opposite its head.

## TURTLE COMPASS
*The needle becomes a magnet when it is stroked by a magnet. As it floats in the bowl, it is affected by the Earth's magnetic field. The turtle's head points to the North and the eye of the needle in its tail points South.*

## BOUNCING CLOWN
*The clown bounces on the invisible magnetic fields of the magnets.*

*The clown's body is hollow so that it is light enough to bounce on the magnets.*

Modelling clay clown

## OPPOSITES ATTRACT...
*The north pole of one magnet and the south pole of another magnet attract (pull towards) each other, and the magnets snap together.*

## ...LIKE POLES REPEL
*Two north poles or two south poles together, repel (push away from) each other, so the magnets 'float' one above the other.*

Modelling clay base

Modelling clay lion

South pole

South pole

Skewer cage bars

*The top magnet will not float if the lion is too heavy.*

North pole

North pole

## LEVITATING LION
Put the magnet with the lion on it in the cage, so that like poles sit on top of each other. The two magnets repel (push away from) each other, making the top magnet float above the bottom one. What happens if you turn the top magnet round, or if you take the cage bars away?

# Making Connections

Batteries can really make things happen! They produce electricity, which can turn a motor or light a bulb. Before the electricity can flow, it must have a path from one side, or terminal, of the battery to the other. This path is called a circuit. On this page you will find out how to connect a battery in a circuit, to light a bulb. You can also make a switch to turn the bulb on and off.

### You will need

Wire

A 4.5V battery

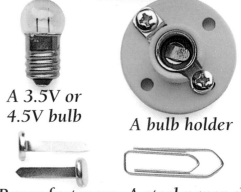

A 3.5V or 4.5V bulb        A bulb holder

Paper fasteners   A steel paper clip

Corrugated cardboard

## Making a simple circuit

1 Cut two pieces of wire, and carefully strip about 2 cm of plastic from their ends. Twist the bare metal strands together.

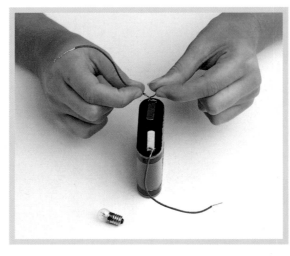

2 Twist a wire tightly around each of the battery terminals, as shown. Make sure that the bare wire is touching the terminal.

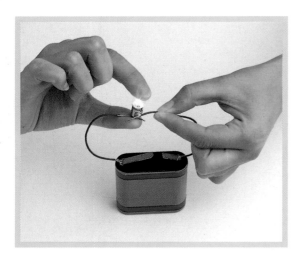

3 Touch one wire to the bottom of the bulb and one to the side. You have made a complete circuit, and the bulb will light up.

4 Screw the bulb into the bulb holder, and attach the wires as shown, using a small screwdriver. The bulb still lights up.

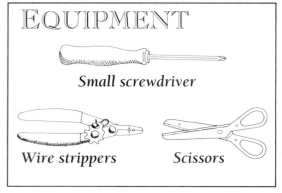

### EQUIPMENT

Small screwdriver

Wire strippers        Scissors

# Making a switch

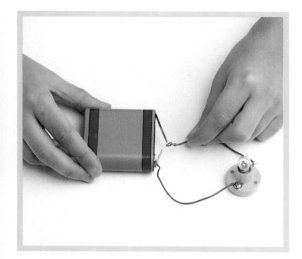

5 Take one of the wires off the battery. The bulb will go out, because there is no longer a complete circuit.

6 Cut another piece of wire. Strip away 2 cm of plastic from each end of the wire and twist the metal strands, as before.

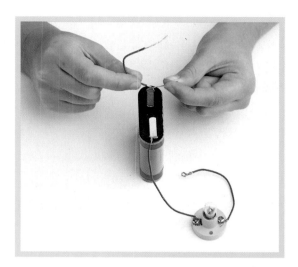

7 Attach one end of the wire to the disconnected terminal of the battery. The other end of the wire will connect to the switch.

8 Carefully cut out a rectangle of cardboard, about 3 cm by 5 cm. This is the base that will hold the pieces you need for the switch.

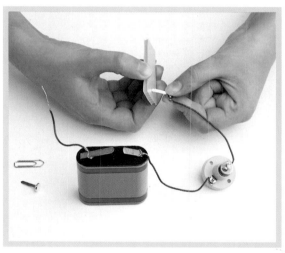

9 Wind the end of the wire from the bulb holder firmly around a paper fastener and push the fastener through the cardboard.

10 Do the same with the end of the other wire, as shown, but this time put a paper clip around the paper fastener as well.

## THE COMPLETED CIRCUIT

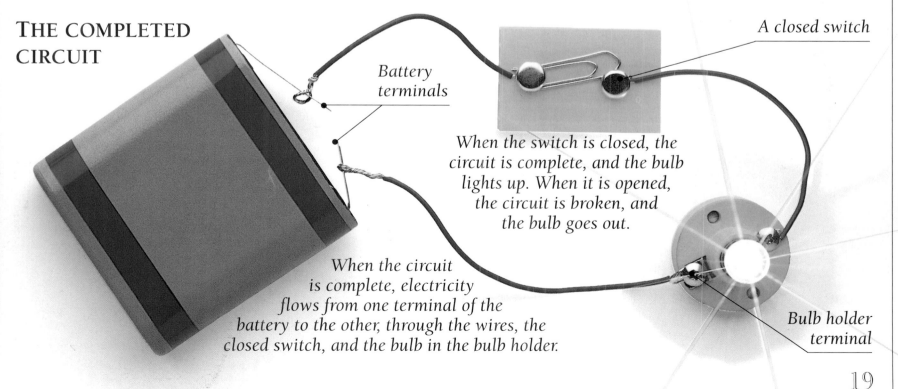

*A closed switch*

*Battery terminals*

*When the switch is closed, the circuit is complete, and the bulb lights up. When it is opened, the circuit is broken, and the bulb goes out.*

*When the circuit is complete, electricity flows from one terminal of the battery to the other, through the wires, the closed switch, and the bulb in the bulb holder.*

*Bulb holder terminal*

19

# HAUNTED HOUSE

With a little imagination, you can transform an old cardboard box and three simple bulb circuits into an eerie, haunted house, full of ghosts that glow in the dark and giant spiders with hairy legs. Find out how to wire up the circuits and decorate the box below. Then, turn the page to see the finished house as the clock strikes midnight, and the haunting begins!

*About*
*1 m of wire*

## You will need

*Three 1.5V bulbs, screwed firmly*
*into three bulb holders*

*Three switches (see page 19)*

*A large*
*cardboard box*

*Sticky tape*

*Three 1.5V batteries*

 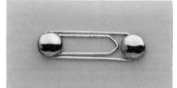 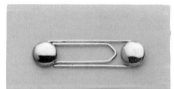

## EQUIPMENT

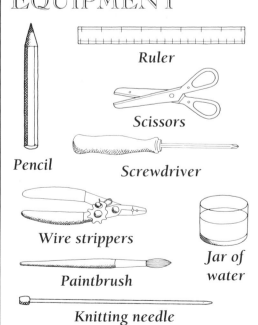

Pencil

Ruler

Scissors

Screwdriver

Wire strippers

Jar of
water

Paintbrush

Knitting needle

## Making the house

1 Tape the top flaps of the box back to the sides. Tape the long flaps together at the bottom and cut off the short flaps*. Paint the box.

2 Connect two stripped wires to each bulb holder. Make a hole in the left side of the box and one in each of the rear bottom corners.

*Save one short flap for the fireplace in step 5.

Pipe cleaners for
making spiders

White and coloured card

Tracing paper

Small
ghost
pattern

Big ghost
pattern
(cut out the
eyes and
the mouth)

Coloured cellophane

Purple
paint

Glue

Coloured felt pens

## Making the furniture

## Making the fire

3 Thread the wires from one bulb holder out through each hole. Connect a switch and a battery to each pair of wires, in a circuit.

4 Draw a fireplace, a portrait, two chairs, a table, and a staircase with a door in it, on white card. Cut them out and colour them in.

5 Paint the spare box flap. Cut a small arch out of it. Cut out flame shapes from the cellophane. Tape them to the back of the arch.

21

# GHOSTS ON GUARD

## Moving in

Tape the fireplace in front of the bulb in the left corner, and the staircase in front of the bulb in the right. Glue the furniture in place.

## Making the spiders

Cut two brown pipe cleaners in half. Wind a black pipe cleaner round the middle of the four halves, as shown. Bend the legs.

## Making the ghosts

Trace the ghost patterns from page 21 onto coloured card and cut them out. Draw eyes and a mouth on the two small ghosts.

## The finished haunted house

*As the clock on the mantelpiece strikes midnight, the ghosts start to prowl...*

### GLOWING GHOUL

*Glue the bulb holder to the wall of the box, then stick the big ghost in front of it, so that the bulb is totally hidden. The ghost glows spookily when the bulb is lit.*

*Glue the switch for each circuit to the sides of the box. Close the switches to make the bulbs light up.*

*The wires are connected to the top and bottom of the battery with tape.*

## SMALL SPOOKS

*Stick the small ghosts to the wall with glue, or suspend them from the ceiling with dark threads.*

*The cellophane flames glow like a real fire when the bulb behind the fireplace is alight.*

## A FAMILY PORTRAIT
*You could glue a small photograph of yourself to the wall instead of drawing a portrait.*

## TERRIFYING TARANTULAS
*Glue the spiders to the box, and bend their legs so they look as though they are scuttling about.*

## IN FULL GLOOM
*The walls, ceiling, and floor are painted a deep purple to make the room look dark and creepy.*

## CREEPY CUPBOARD
*Stick a small ghost to the back of one door, as though it is escaping from the cupboard under the stairs.*

*This switch controls the bulb hidden behind the cupboard doors.*

*Tape the table and chairs firmly to the floor of the box with dark tape.*

*Open the cupboard doors under the stairs to let an eerie light shine through.*

23

# STOCK CARS

Did you know that a car's lights are powered by a battery? The lights are connected in two different types of circuit. Headlights are connected 'in series' (the bulbs are wired together, one after the other, in a circuit). The indicators are connected 'in parallel' (two separate circuits are connected to the same battery). Here you can find out how to make a 'smashing' stock car with working headlights and indicators.

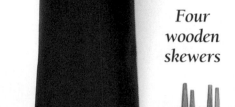

*About 1 m of wire*

## You will need

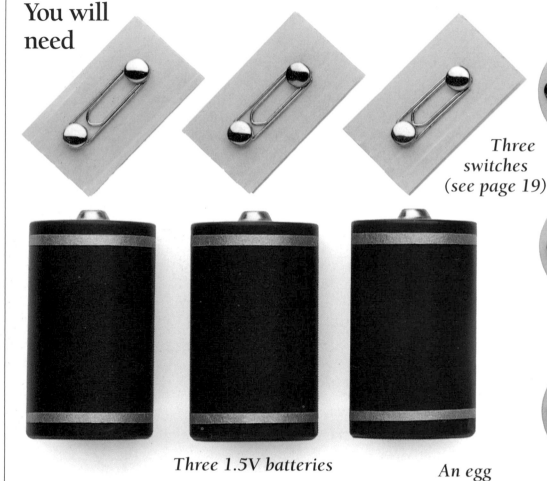

*Three switches (see page 19)*

*Glue*

*Four wooden skewers*

*Three 1.5V batteries*

*An egg box*

*Four 1.5V bulbs in bulb holders*

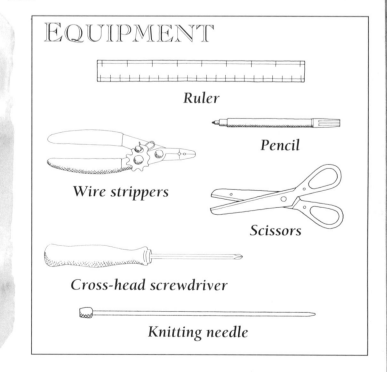

EQUIPMENT

*Ruler*

*Pencil*

*Wire strippers*

*Scissors*

*Cross-head screwdriver*

*Knitting needle*

24

*A shoe box, with its lid*

*Four model car wheels, or circles of stiff card*

*Coloured card*

*Sticky tape*

*Aluminium foil*

# Making the car body

1 Cut away the box, as shown, making sure that the long sides of the car are the same*. Tape the back flap to the sides of the car.

2 Cut down the box lid to fit the top of the car and a windscreen. Fold down the cut end to make the windscreen, and tape it in place**.

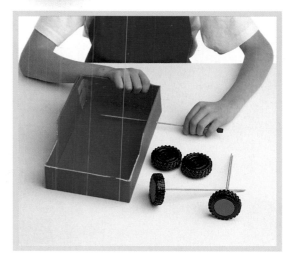

3 Push a wheel on to each pair of skewers. Make holes for axles: two holes at the rear of the car and two below the windscreen*.

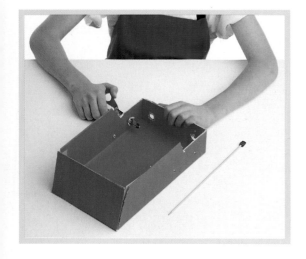

4 Make two holes, large enough for a bulb to go through, in the front of the car. Then, make a hole on either side of the bonnet.

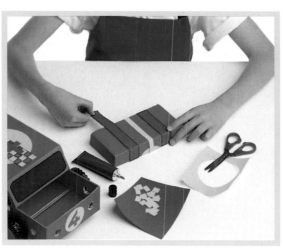

5 Poke the skewers through the axle holes and push wheels on to the ends. Decorate the stock car with pieces of coloured paper

6 Cover two cups from an egg box with foil. Make a big hole in the bottom of each, then glue one over each headlight hole.

*Ask an adult to help you with this.

**The piece of lid left over becomes the car's bonnet.

25

# LIGHTING-UP TIME

## Headlights 'in series'

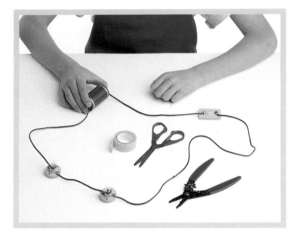
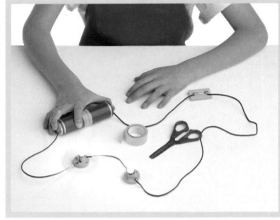

## Indicators 'in parallel'

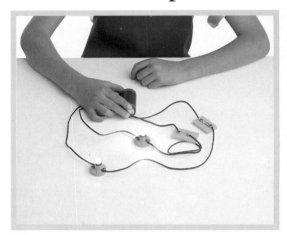

1 Connect two bulbs 'in series' in a circuit, as shown. The lights are dim as one battery is too weak to power two bulbs wired in series.

2 Tape the top of one battery to the bottom of another, in series. Connect the batteries to the circuit, as shown. Now the lights are bright.

3 Connect two separate circuits, each with a bulb and a switch, to one battery, as shown. Bulbs wired in parallel shine brightly.

## Stock car smash-up

*The car headlights are wired in series because both lights need to be on at the same time. Indicators are used one at a time, so they are wired in parallel, with separate switches.*

*Glue a large paper number to the roof, sides and bonnet of your stock car.*

### BRIGHT LIGHTS!
*Foil cups around the headlights reflect the light forward from the bulbs. This makes the headlights appear brighter.*

# Fitting the lights

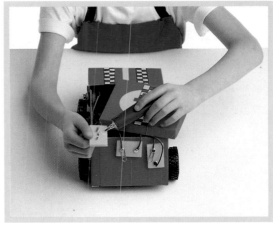

1 Put the headlights circuit into the car. Glue the switch to the back of the car. Push one bulb through each foil cup, as shown.

2 Glue a foil-covered card circle over both side holes. Make a big hole in each, as before. Push an indicator bulb through each hole.

3 Put the circuit in the car. Glue the left indicator switch to the left side of the car and the right indicator switch to the right side.

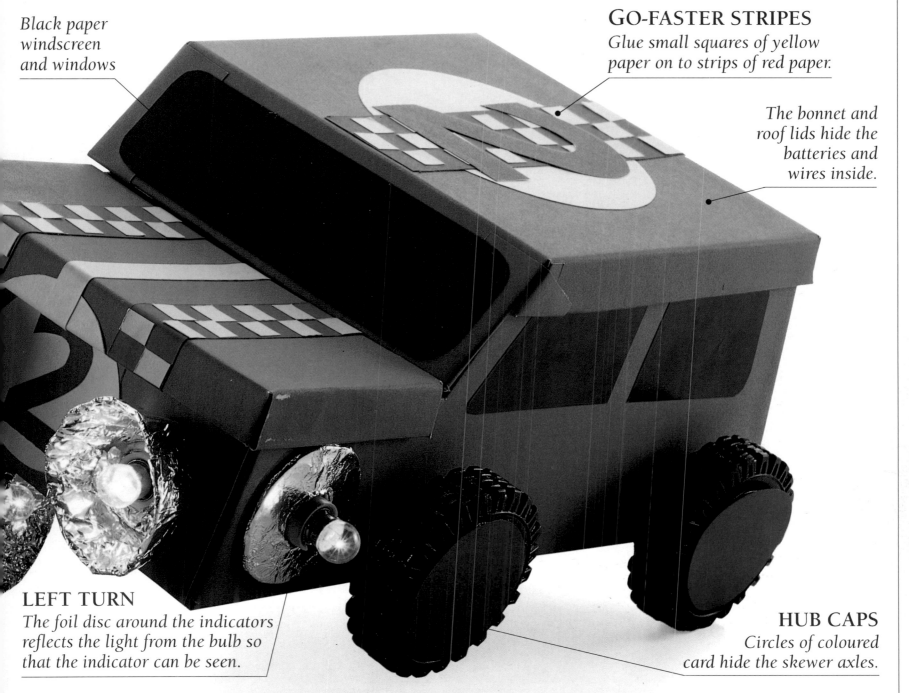

*Black paper windscreen and windows*

## GO-FASTER STRIPES
*Glue small squares of yellow paper on to strips of red paper.*

*The bonnet and roof lids hide the batteries and wires inside.*

## LEFT TURN
*The foil disc around the indicators reflects the light from the bulb so that the indicator can be seen.*

## HUB CAPS
*Circles of coloured card hide the skewer axles.*

27

# BUG PROBES

Electricity can flow through some materials but not others. It can't flow through plastic, so you must strip the plastic from the ends of a wire to make a connection. Materials that let electricity flow through them are called conductors. Make a battery bug probe, then look for conductors around your home.

*Two 1.5V batteries*

*A 4.5V battery*

## You will need

*Some sequins*

*Three pipe cleaners*

*A bulb holder*

*A 3.5V bulb*   *Two 2.5V bulbs*

*Flex or wire*

*Some coloured card and paper*

### EQUIPMENT

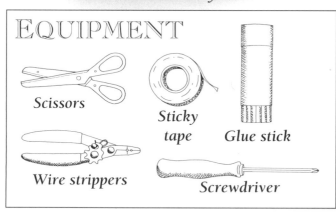

*Scissors*

*Sticky tape*   *Glue stick*

*Wire strippers*   *Screwdriver*

*Aluminium foil*

## Making the leggy bug

1 Put a square of foil between the top of one 1.5V battery and the bottom of the other, as shown. Tape the batteries firmly together.

3 Screw the 3.5V bulb into the holder. Connect the 12 cm and 8 cm wires to the holder. Tape the 8 cm wire to the top of the battery.

## Making the smiley bug

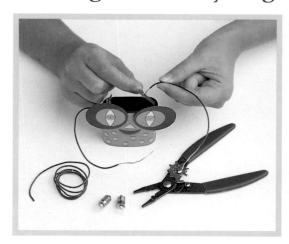

1 Decorate the 4.5V battery with coloured paper. Cut two wires and strip their ends. Attach a wire to each of the battery terminals.

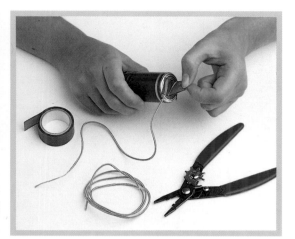

## Leggy bug

*Decorate the body of the bug with tiny circles of coloured paper and card.*

*Coloured sequins glued on to two ovals of card*

*Tape pipe cleaner legs to the underside of the bug.*

2 Cut a 25 cm, a 12 cm, and an 8 cm length of wire and strip their ends. Connect the 25 cm wire to the bottom of the battery.

*Aluminium foil is a good conductor of electricity.*

*Wire antennae with aluminium foil balls at the stripped ends*

4 Tape the holder to the batteries. Wrap them in paper with the two free wires sticking out at the top. Push foil balls on to the wires.

## BUG CONDUCTORS

*Touch the bulbs of the smiley bug, or the foil balls of the leggy bug, to different materials around your home. The bulbs will light up, if the material conducts electricity.*

## Smiley bug

*Touch the bottoms of the bulbs to the object being tested.*

*Coloured paper and sequin eyes*

2 Wind each wire round a screwdriver, to make it curly. Twist the end of each wire firmly around a 2.5V bulb, as shown.

## WHAT HAPPENS

*When you touch the bug's antennae together, or to a material that conducts electricity, the bulb lights up because the circuit is complete. When you touch them to a material that doesn't conduct electricity, the circuit is broken and the light goes out.*

# Battery Power

Making your own battery is electrifyingly easy! All you need is some coins, some tissues, a lemon and some aluminium foil. Then you can light a special, coloured bulb, called an LED (Light Emitting Diode). LEDs only light up when connected one way round, so follow the instructions carefully!

## You will need

Aluminium foil

Coloured card

A lemon

Some coins

Some wire

Sticky tape

## Wiring an LED

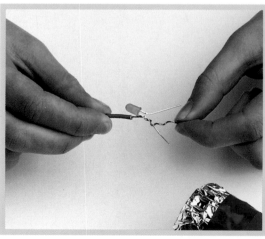

Gently, bend the legs of the LED apart. Attach the stripped end of a wire to each leg of the LED by twisting it round, as shown.

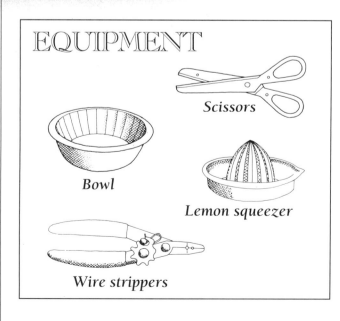

Some paper tissues

### EQUIPMENT

Scissors

Bowl

Lemon squeezer

Wire strippers

Long, positive leg

Short, negative leg

An LED
(Light Emmitting Diode)

## Making the battery

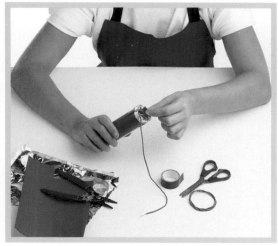

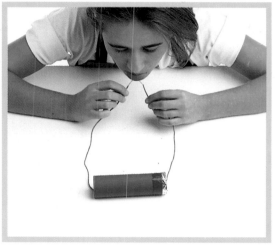

## Completing the circuit

1 Make a tube from card. Wrap some foil over one end, and tape it to the tube. Strip ends of a wire and tape one end to the foil.

2 Squeeze the lemon, then soak the tissues in its juice. Build up repeating layers of first a tissue, then a coin and then a piece of foil

3 Finish your battery on a coin layer, then tape the stripped end of another wire to it. Touch the two wires to your tongue.

## The finished battery

*Below you can see a cut-away of a finished battery, with its repeating layers visible, and a complete battery, with its LED glowing.*

*The long leg of the LED is connected to the positive terminal of the battery.*

*Short leg of the LED is attached to the negative terminal of the battery.*

### INSIDE THE BATTERY

*Repeating layers, from the bottom of the battery, of tissue soaked in lemon juice, then a coin, then a piece of foil.*

*Positive coin terminal*

*The LED may not glow brightly if your battery is not very powerful.*

*Make sure that the wires wrapped round the legs of the LED do not touch each other, or the LED won't light.*

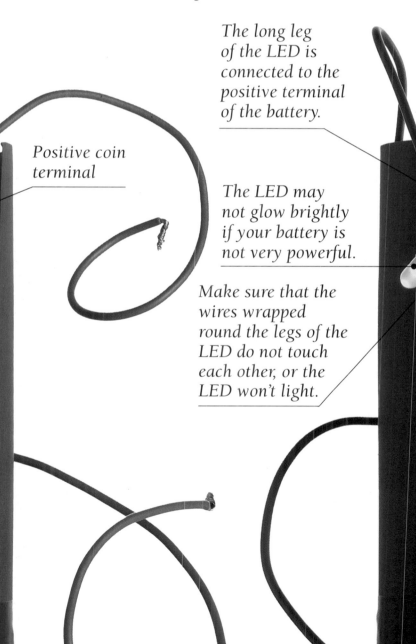

*Negative foil terminal*

*Wire taped to the foil*

31

# ROBOT MASK

Surprise your friends with an amazing robot mask, that glows in the dark! Its small red LED lights only light up one way round, so always connect the shorter leg of the LED to the negative $-$ terminal of the battery and the longer leg to the positive $+$ terminal. Make sure that the wires from the LEDs are long enough to let you hide the switch and batteries in your pocket.

## EQUIPMENT

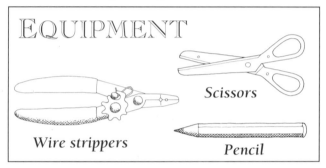

Wire strippers

Scissors

Pencil

Eight LEDs

Nuts and washers

A switch (see page 19)

(see page 19)

### You will need

1.5 m of wire

Coloured, shiny paper and white card

Black paper

Aluminium foil

String or elastic

Sticky tape

Two 9V batteries

A glue stick

## Making the mask

1 Cut out a mask shape in black paper. Stick it on to white card. Cut slots for the eyes and the LEDs. Make holes for the string.

2 Decorate your mask with the coloured paper, washers and nuts. Thread a string through each hole and knot it, as shown.

3 Glue together a strip of paper and card, just larger than the LED slot. Make eight evenly spaced holes. Push LEDs through.

# Connecting the LEDs

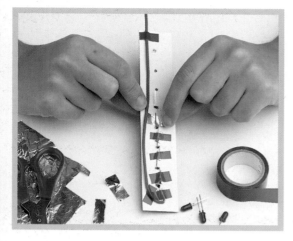

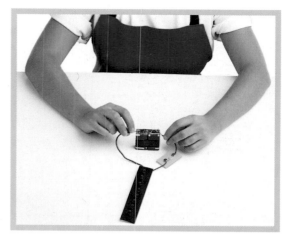

4 Bend the LEDs' legs apart.* Wrap foil tightly round the short leg of one LED and the long leg of the next, and tape to card.**

5 Tape the batteries together so that the ⊕ terminal of one is next to the ⊖ of the other. Tape foil over the middle terminals.

6 Connect the switch, batteries and LEDs in a circuit. Which way round do the LEDs work? Tape the LED strip to the mask.

## The finished mask

Ask someone to help you tie the string or elastic tightly at the back of your head to hold the mask in place.

*Make sure that the wires from the mask are long enough to reach the batteries and switch hidden in your pocket.*

*Black paper*

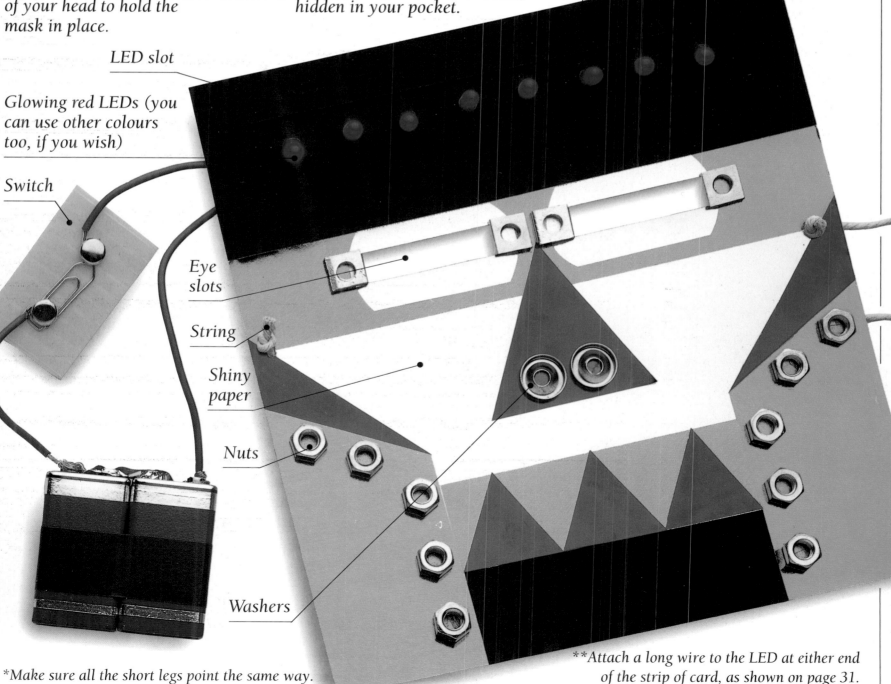

*LED slot*

*Glowing red LEDs (you can use other colours too, if you wish)*

*Switch*

*Eye slots*

*String*

*Shiny paper*

*Nuts*

*Washers*

*Make sure all the short legs point the same way.

**Attach a long wire to the LED at either end of the strip of card, as shown on page 31.

# MOTOR MANIA

Electricity can do a lot more than light bulbs. If you connect a battery to an electric motor, you can make things move too! Here, and on the next two pages, you can find out how to make colourful fans to keep you cool, and a spectacular, whirling merry-go-round.

*Cotton bud*

*Pipe cleaners*

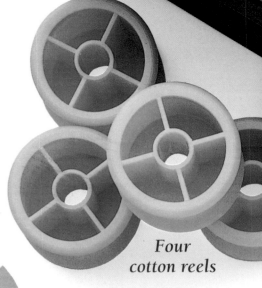

*Four cotton reels*

## You will need

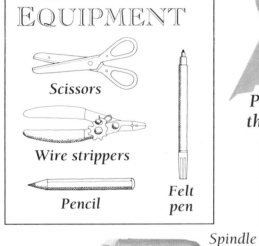

### EQUIPMENT

*Scissors*

*Wire strippers*

*Pencil*

*Felt pen*

*Pattern for the vultures*

*A switch (see page 19)*

*A 1.5V battery*

*Pattern for the swallows*

*Pattern for the fans*

*Spindle*

*Motor terminals*

*A 1.5V-4V electric motor*

## Connecting the motor

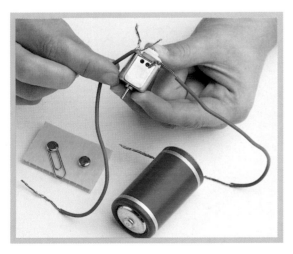

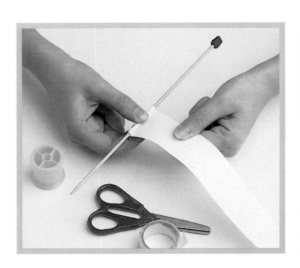

1 Connect a stripped wire to each terminal of the motor, as shown*. Cut a stem from a cotton bud. Push it on to the spindle.

2 Connect motor in a circuit, as shown. Glue the motor to the box, so that the top of the spindle is level with the top of the box.

3 To make a 'sleeve', roll a strip of paper around the knitting needle. The sleeve must fit snugly into the centre of one cotton reel.

34     *Divide the end of the wire in half, thread one half through the terminal, then twist the two halves together.*

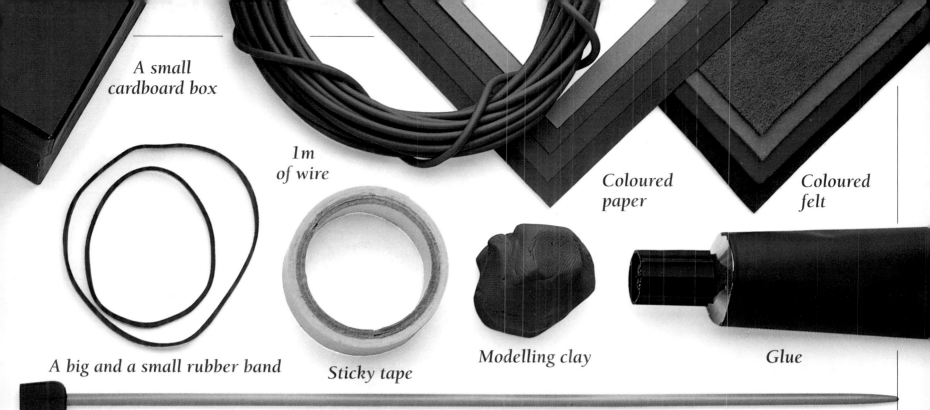

A small
cardboard box

1m
of wire

Coloured
paper

Coloured
felt

A big and a small rubber band

Sticky tape

Modelling clay

Glue

A knitting needle

# Making the merry-go-round

4 Stick the three other reels in place on the needle with the clay, as shown. Glue the reel with a sleeve to the bottom of the box.

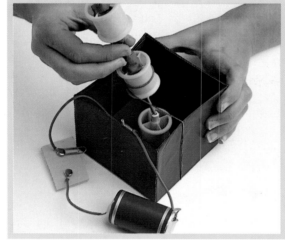

5 Stretch the big rubber band round the box. Put the small band on to the reel which is third from the top of the needle, as shown.

6 Use three pipe cleaners for each bird - one for the head and body, and one for each wing. Bend vultures' heads, as shown.

7 Trace the vulture and swallow patterns, then cut them out in coloured felt. Stick the birds to the six pipe cleaner bodies with tape.

8 Tape a pipe cleaner to each bird, then tape all the birds to the top two reels, as shown. Stand the needle in the reel, in the box.

9 Glue a ring of card to the top reel. Stretch the small band on to the spindle. Make sure the tops of the motor and reel are level**

** Adjust the cotton reel with the band on it as necessary.

35

# FAN-TASTIC

## Making a fan

1 Cut out a card fan, using the pattern on page 34. Decorate it with coloured paper. Make a hole in the middle of the fan with a pencil.

2 Connect a switch, motor, and battery together in a circuit. Push a tube cut from the stem of a cotton bud onto the motor.

3 Push the fan shape onto the spindle. Stick it in place with modelling clay. Bend the card up, as shown, to make the fan blades.

## WHIRLING MERRY-GO-ROUND

*Add the finishing touches to your merry-go-round by putting the battery in one corner of the box, where it won't be seen. Then, glue the switch to the outside, where you can turn it on and off easily.*

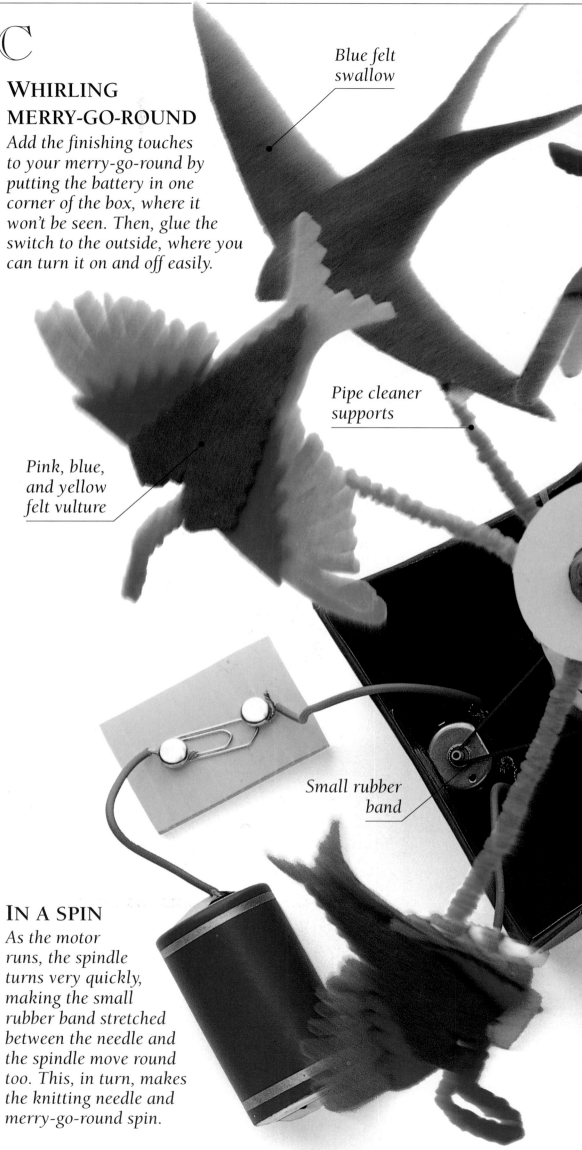

Blue felt swallow

Pipe cleaner supports

Pink, blue, and yellow felt vulture

Small rubber band

## IN A SPIN

*As the motor runs, the spindle turns very quickly, making the small rubber band stretched between the needle and the spindle move round too. This, in turn, makes the knitting needle and merry-go-round spin.*

## COOL IT!

*The folded blades of the fan push the air out of the way as they whizz round, producing a lovely, cooling breeze.*

*Pink and blue felt vulture*

## ADJUSTER

*Adjust the big rubber band around the box to keep the knitting needle vertical. This will stop the small rubber band slipping off the motor.*

## FAN FUN

*Now you have made your fan, you can start experimenting with it. Find out what happens if you connect the battery the other way round in the circuit. Try folding the fan blades up in the other direction. What happens to the amount of breeze the fan produces?*

*Big rubber band*

*Experiment by decorating fan blades with different colours and patterns, then watch how they change as the fans spin round.*

37

# ELECTROMAGNETS

You can make magnets with electricity, too. They are called electromagnets and, unlike ordinary magnets, their magnetic powers can be switched on and off. All you need is a battery, some wire, a screwdriver and a switch. The experiment works best if the screwdriver has an iron shaft, but a steel shaft will do.

**You will need**

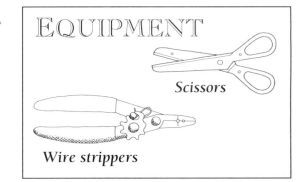
*About 2 m of wire*

*Sticky tape*

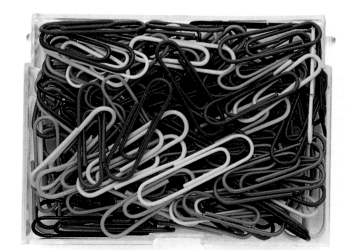

*A switch (see page 19)*

*A 4.5V battery*

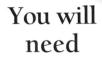
*Lots of paper clips*

*A long screwdriver*

## What to do

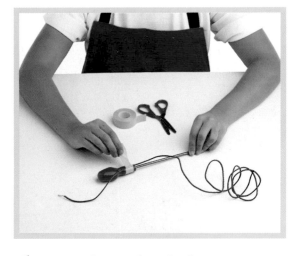

1 Strip the ends of a long piece of wire. Tape one end to the handle of a screwdriver, leaving the other end of the wire free.

2 Wind the wire tightly around the screwdriver 20, 40, or 60 times. Tape the last turn of the wire firmly to the screwdriver.

3 Connect the switch, battery, and screwdriver in a circuit, as shown. How many paper clips can each electromagnet pick up?

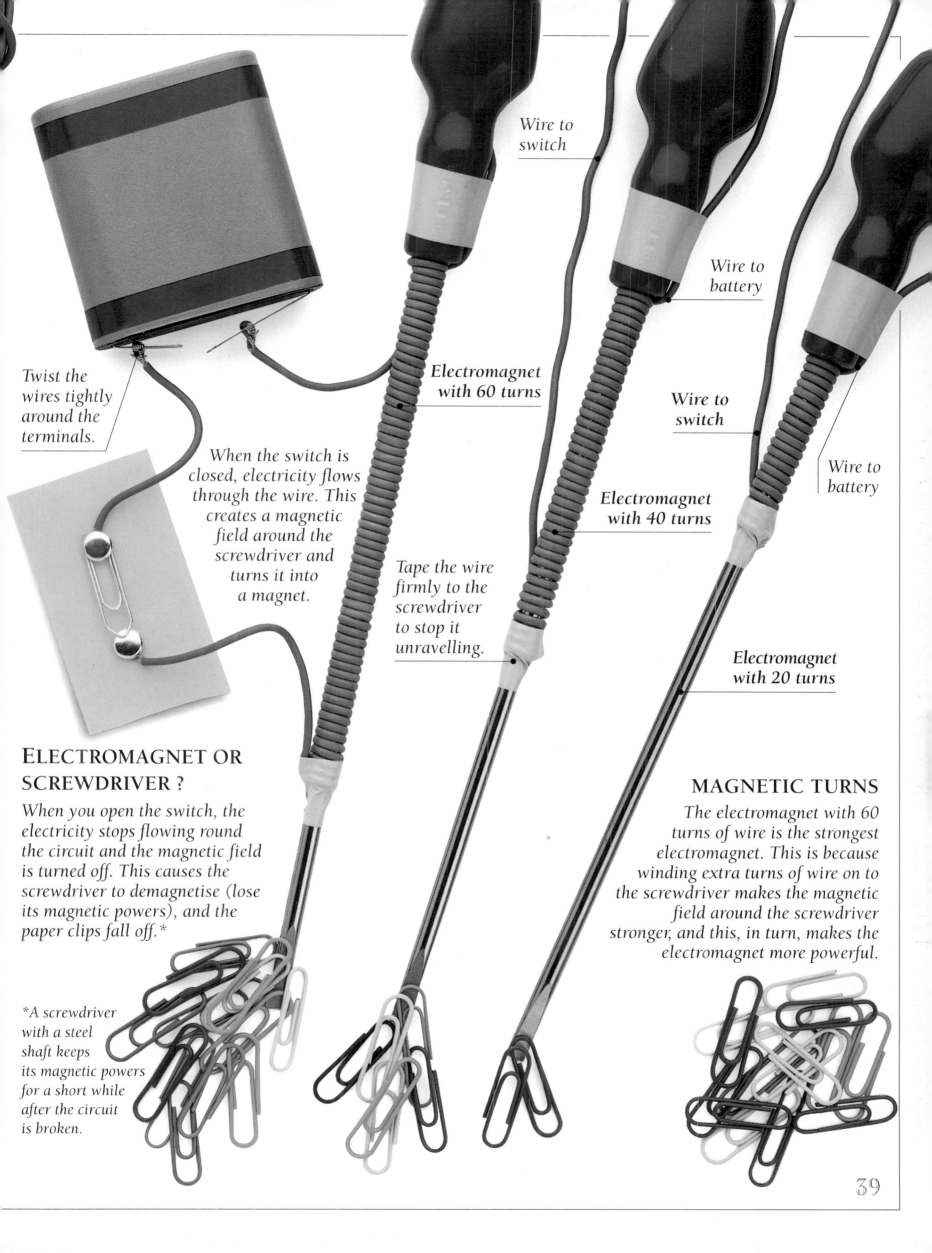

Wire to switch

Wire to battery

Wire to switch

Wire to battery

Twist the wires tightly around the terminals.

When the switch is closed, electricity flows through the wire. This creates a magnetic field around the screwdriver and turns it into a magnet.

Electromagnet with 60 turns

Tape the wire firmly to the screwdriver to stop it unravelling.

Electromagnet with 40 turns

Electromagnet with 20 turns

## ELECTROMAGNET OR SCREWDRIVER ?

When you open the switch, the electricity stops flowing round the circuit and the magnetic field is turned off. This causes the screwdriver to demagnetise (lose its magnetic powers), and the paper clips fall off.*

*A screwdriver with a steel shaft keeps its magnetic powers for a short while after the circuit is broken.

## MAGNETIC TURNS

The electromagnet with 60 turns of wire is the strongest electromagnet. This is because winding extra turns of wire on to the screwdriver makes the magnetic field around the screwdriver stronger, and this, in turn, makes the electromagnet more powerful.

# BUSY BUZZER

Once you know how to make an electromagnet (see page 38), you can build this noisy buzzer. The handle of the nail-file and the paint on the drinks can don't conduct electricity, so make sure that wires are only connected to bare metal, or the buzzer won't work. Look at the photograph of the buzzer circuit, as you follow the steps, to check that you have put everything in the right place.

**You will need**

*A 4.5V battery*

*A metal drinks can*

*Corrugated cardboard*

*A steel nail-file*

*A switch (see page 19)*

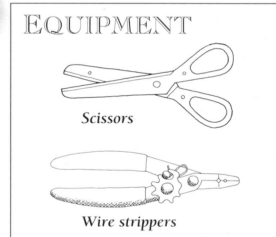

*Modelling clay*

*A cotton reel*

*A rubber band*

*Wire (at least 3 m long)*

*Sticky tape*

*An iron or steel bolt*

## EQUIPMENT

*Scissors*

*Wire strippers*

## Making the buzzer

1 Wrap the wire firmly around the bolt 200 times. Strip both ends of the wire. Stick the bolt to the cardboard with modelling clay.

2 Attach the nail-file to the cotton reel with the rubber band, as shown. Make sure that the nail-file is held tightly in place.

3 Use the scissors to scratch away two squares of paint, along the bottom edge, on opposite sides of the drinks can.

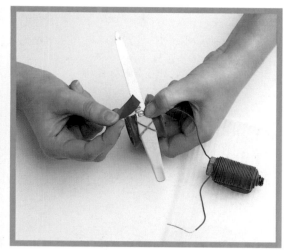  

4 Firmly tape a wire from the bolt to the metal part of the nail-file, as shown. Stick the cotton reel in place on the card with clay.

5 Cut a short piece of wire and strip its ends. Attach one end to the battery. Tape the other to one of the scratched squares on the can.

6 Stick the can to the card with clay, so that the other square touches the nail-file. Connect the bolt to a switch, then to the battery.

## BUZZING ABOUT

*When you close the switch, electricity flows around the circuit. The bolt becomes an electromagnet and pulls the nail-file away from the can. This breaks the circuit, so* *that the electromagnet loses its power and the nail-file springs back, hits the can, and completes the circuit again. This process happens over and over, very quickly.*

### CAN-CAN
*You may need to adjust the position of the can to make the buzzer work. The nail-file should just touch the scratched square on one side of the can.*

*The steel nail-file is attracted to the electromagnet.*

### FINE TUNING
*Make sure that the end of the bolt is opposite the bare steel of the nail-file. If, at first, the buzzer won't work, move the cotton reel so that the nail-file is nearer to the bolt.*

*Push the bolt firmly into the modelling clay so that the wire can't unwind.*

### CONTACT!
*The buzzing noise is made by the nail-file hitting the can very quickly, over and over again. Watch out for flying sparks, too!*

*Open the switch to stop the buzzer.*

41

# MAKING A RADIO

Have you ever wanted to make your own radio and not known where to start? Here and on the next five pages, you can find out what to do! Follow the instructions very carefully, as this project is quite difficult. Everything you will need to make the radio is shown below. There are tips on where to buy the components on page 48, but don't worry if the ones you buy don't look exactly the same as the components we have used.

*Corrugated cardboard*

## EQUIPMENT

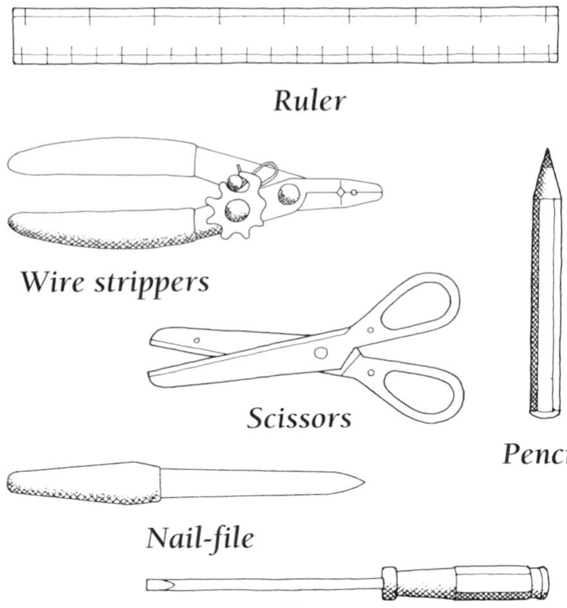

*Ruler*

*Wire strippers*

*Scissors*

*Pencil*

*Nail-file*

*Small screwdriver*

*A shoe box*

## You will need

*A diode*

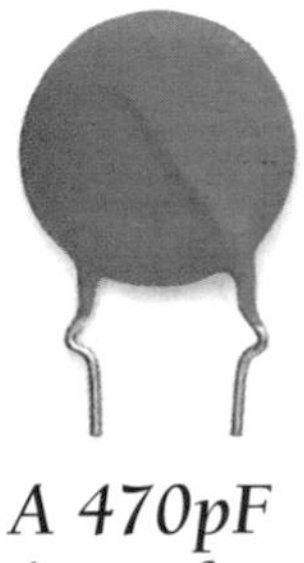

*A 470pF (pico-farad) capacitor*

*Two 3.3kΩ (kilo-ohm) resistors*

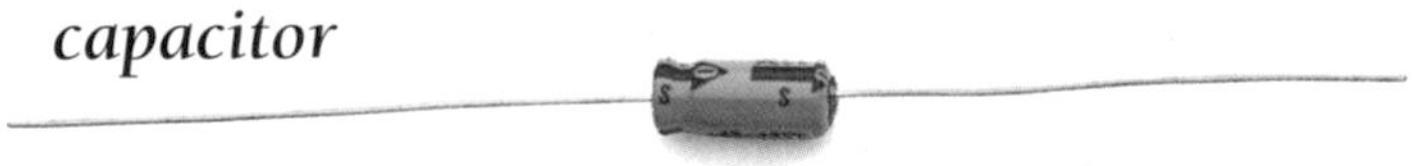

*A 3.3μF (micro-farad) electrolytic capacitor*

*A 10kΩ resistor*

*A 22kΩ resistor*

*A 10kΩ variable resistor*

*Two general purpose PNP transistors*

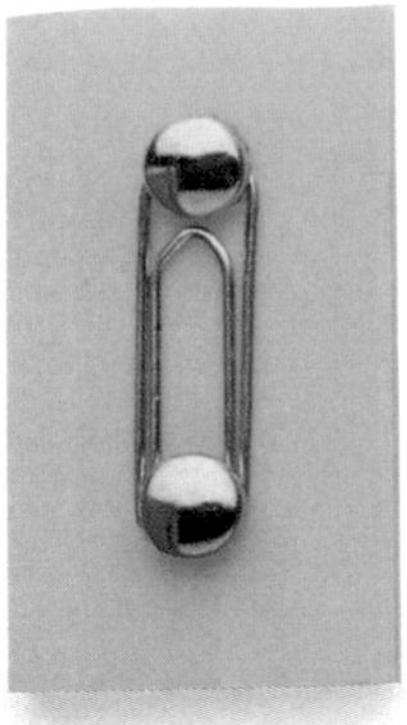

*A switch (see page 19)*

*A 9V battery*

*An earphone (sometimes called a crystal earpiece)*

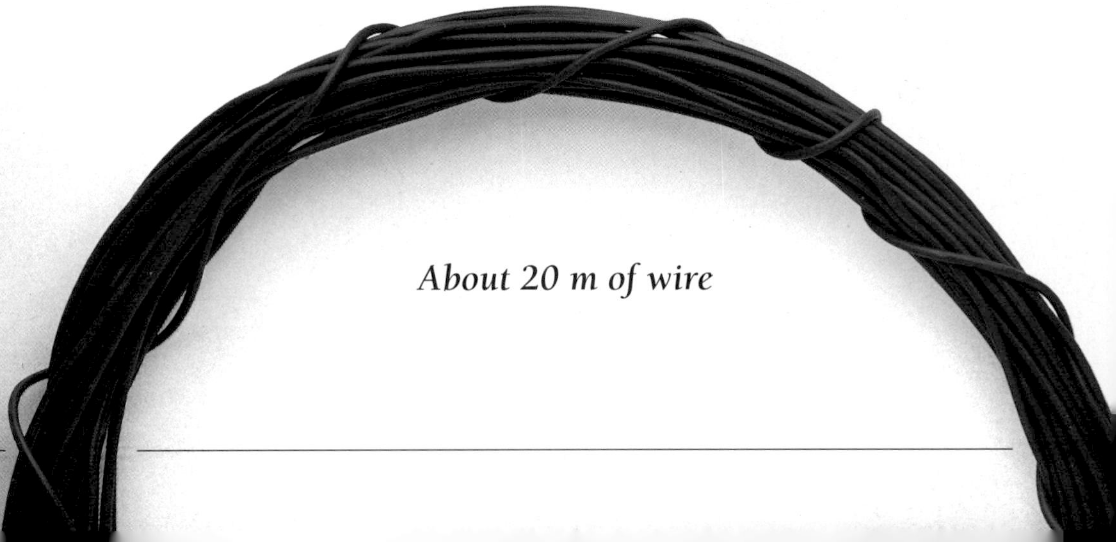

*About 20 m of wire*

Kitchen foil

Coloured paper

*Sticky tape*

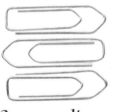

*3 paper clips*

*2 paper fasteners*

A strip of 12 screw connectors

*A cotton reel*

*25-30 gauge magnet winding wire or resin-coated copper wire (for the receiving coil)*

*Glue*

## Preparing the box

1 Draw a rectangle, the same size as the cotton reel lying on its side, on one end of the box. Carefully cut out the rectangle.

2 Make two holes in the front of the box, as shown. The larger hole is for the volume knob, and the small one is for the earphone.

## Aerial and earth wires

3 Cut out shapes from coloured paper and foil for decoration. Glue the shapes onto the box to make it look like a radio.

## Making a coil

4 Cut one wire 10 m long, and another 5 m long. Strip one end of each wires and attach a fastener to each one.

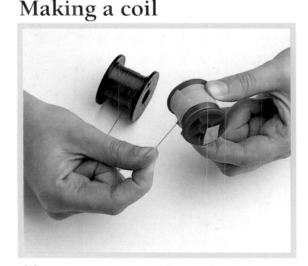

5 Wrap tape, sticky-side out, round the reel. Carefully wind the fine wire on to the reel, making each turn very close to the last.

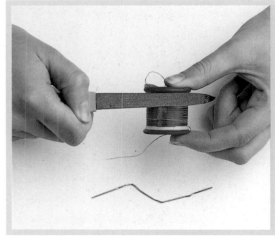

6 File the coating from one end of the fine wire and from a strip along the coil, as shown. Bend a paper clip for a tuning arm.

# Radio Workshop

On the opposite page, you can see all the components connected up to make the radio circuit. Use it as a guide as you set out your circuit. The steps show you how to make each type of connection. Some components have to be connected the right way round, so if you can't tell which leg of a component is which, ask at the shop where you bought it. Turn the page to see the finished radio.

## Starting off

Cut a rectangle of cardboard to fit in the bottom of the box. Cut the strip of connectors into nine single blocks and one block of three.

## Connecting the diode

## Screw connectors

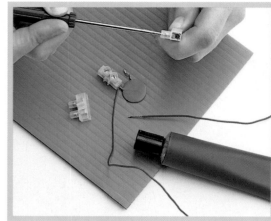

Partially undo the screw in one half of the screw connector. Push a wire and/or a component leg into the hole left by the screw.

## Connecting transistors

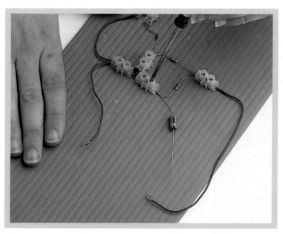

Wind the screw back into the connector. Check connection is firm by tugging each component. Glue the connector to the card.

## Electrolytic capacitor

The diode must be connected the right way round in the circuit. The end with a black line is connected to the transistor.

## Variable resistor

A transistor has three legs: a base, an emitter and a collector*. Bend the legs apart, as shown. Screw each leg into its connector.

## Connecting the battery

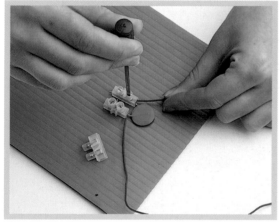

Connect the negative leg of the electrolytic capacitor (marked with an arrow or a minus sign) to the transistor's collector, as shown.

Attach one of the wires from the block of three screw connectors to each of the three terminals of the variable resistor, as shown.

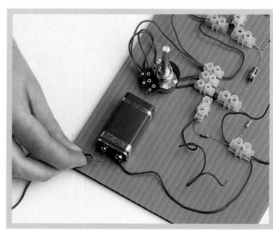

Make sure that the battery is connected the right way, so that the wire from the positive terminal is connected to the switch.

*The instructions that come with your transistors will tell you how to find out which leg is which.

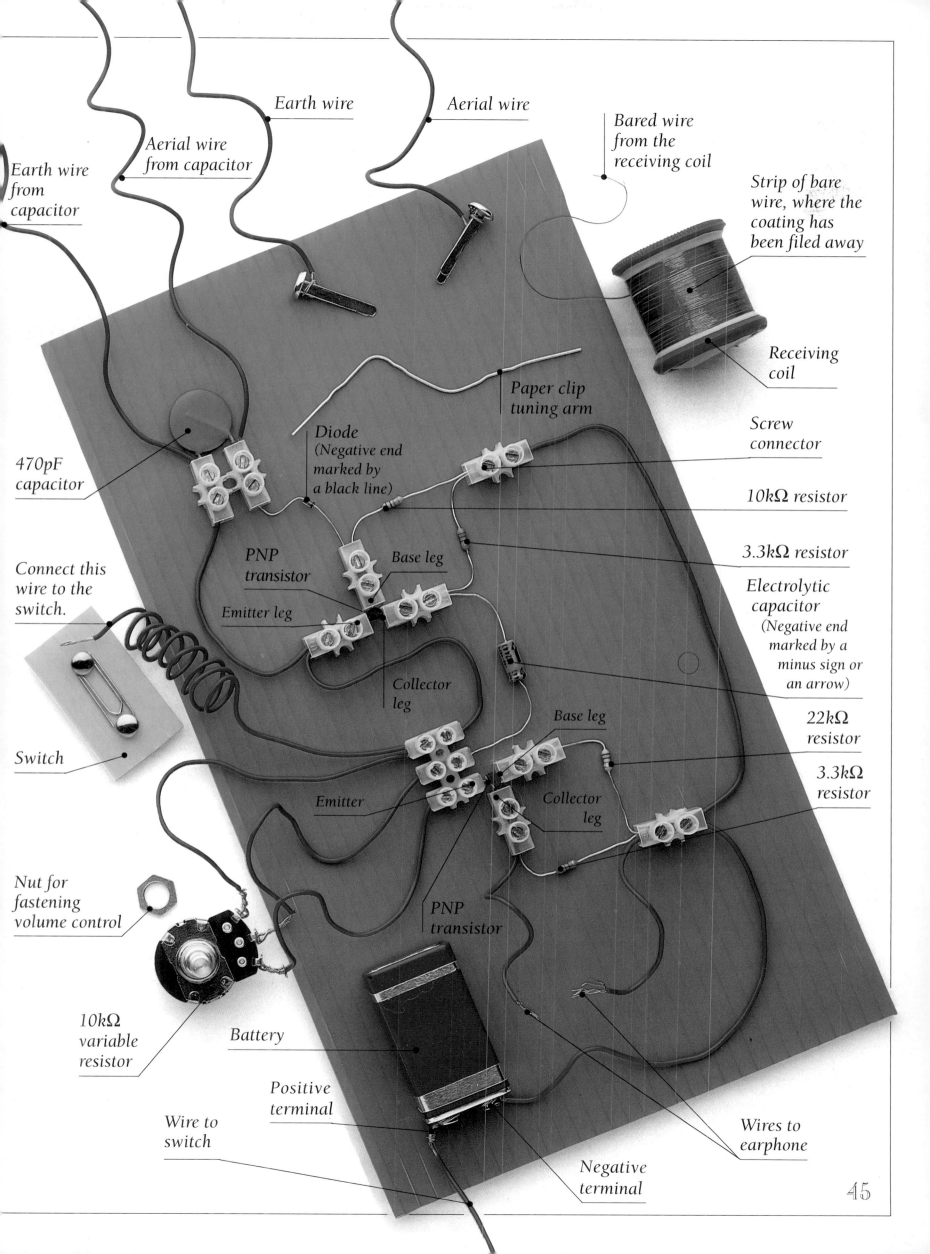

Earth wire

Aerial wire

Bared wire
from the
receiving coil

Aerial wire
from capacitor

Strip of bare
wire, where the
coating has
been filed away

Earth wire
from
capacitor

Receiving
coil

Screw
connector

Diode
(Negative end
marked by
a black line)

Paper clip
tuning arm

470pF
capacitor

10kΩ resistor

3.3kΩ resistor

PNP
transistor

Base leg

Electrolytic
capacitor
(Negative end
marked by a
minus sign or
an arrow)

Connect this
wire to the
switch.

Emitter leg

22kΩ
resistor

Collector
leg

Base leg

3.3kΩ
resistor

Switch

Emitter

Collector
leg

Nut for
fastening
volume control

PNP
transistor

10kΩ
variable
resistor

Battery

Wires to
earphone

Positive
terminal

Wire to
switch

Negative
terminal

45

# ON THE AIR

## Finishing off

 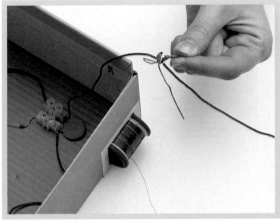 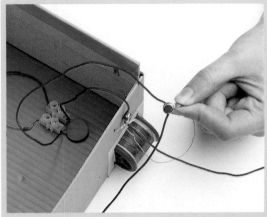

1 Put the circuit into the box. Tape the coil halfway through the hole so that the bared wire and the filed strip are outside the box.

2 Bend the tuning arm around the earth wire's paper fastener, as shown. Attach the earth wire from the capacitor to the paper fastener.

3 Attach the capacitor's aerial wire and coil's bare wire to the aerial wire's paper fastener. Push fasteners through box, as below.

## Tuning the radio

Once you have finished making the radio, you are ready to tune in to the airwaves! First, put the earphone in your ear, very carefully. Then, move the tuning arm slowly along the bare wire of the receiving coil. As you push the arm over the coil, you should be able to tune in to several different radio stations. The more turns of wire there are on the coil, the more radio stations you will be able to pick up.

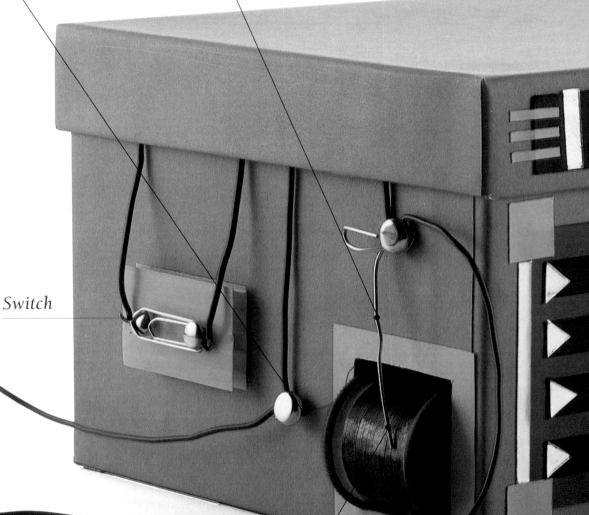

*Wire from receiving coil to aerial wire*

*Paper clip tuning-arm*

*Switch*

### AERIAL
*The aerial works best when it is hung in the air in a straight line, with some of it out of doors. This way, it can catch as much of the radio signal as possible.*

### EARTH WIRE
*Strip 15 cm of plastic from the end of the earth wire, then attach the end to a metal sink tap.*

*Bend the tuning arm so that it touches the bared wire of the coil, very firmly.*

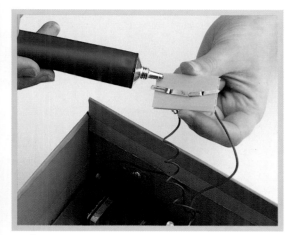

4 Connect the spare wire from the battery to the switch. Glue the switch to the outside of the box, beside the receiving coil.

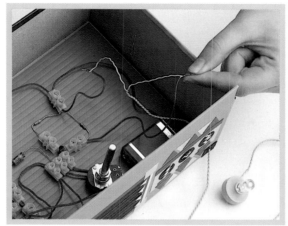

5 Push both earphone wires through the hole in the box. Connect one of them to each of the free wires from the 3.3kΩ resistor.

6 Push the variable resistor arm through its hole and screw the nut on tightly. Wind tape round the knob, as shown, to decorate it.

## TUNING BAND

*Make a tuning display panel from pieces of coloured paper and aluminium foil.*

*Screw the nut on tightly, so that the volume knob is held firmly in place.*

## VOLUME CONTROL

*Turn the knob up for very quiet or faint stations, and down for very loud or strong ones. Never listen to a loud radio station with the sound turned up high, as you may damage your hearing.*

*Push the earphone wire back into the box when you finish listening to the radio.*

## LISTENING IN

*The invisible radio waves, which carry the signals of radio stations through the air, are made of electricity and magnetism! They are picked up by the radio's aerial. Tuning the radio selects the signal from one radio station and makes it stronger. The earphone changes the signal into sound, so that you can hear it.*

# CHECKLIST

If you have any problems getting your electrical circuits to work, try checking the following things:

1 Always check that you have connected each component and wire of the circuit exactly as you have been shown.

2 Make sure that connections made with tape or kitchen foil are tight enough, by pressing them together firmly.

3 Check that no component, foil connection, or stray wire in one part of the circuit is touching another part by accident, as the electricity will miss out components or maybe even the whole circuit. This problem is called a short-circuit.

4 If a circuit stays on when the switch is open, make sure that the paper fasteners are not touching underneath the switch.

5 If you have checked all of the above, and your circuit still doesn't work, try replacing the batteries.

6 If your circuit still doesn't work, one or more of the components could be faulty. In the radio, this is most likely to be the transistors. Try replacing them.

# SUPPLIERS

If you have trouble finding any of the components or equipment needed for projects in this book, try contacting the suppliers suggested below.

**Hardware or general electrical shops** - screwdrivers, wire strippers, wire, batteries, motors, bulb holders, bulbs, magnets, strip connectors, nuts, bolts, washers.
**Electronics components shops and suppliers** (Try electronics shops, television repairers, or look in the phone book and electronics magazines for names and addresses of local suppliers)- components for the radio, wire, hook-up wire, LEDs.
**Model and craft shops** - motors, felt, pipe cleaners, corrugated plastic.
**Toy shops** - iron filings, magnets.